HURRICANES
AND TYPHOONS

This edition produced in 1995
© Aladdin Books Ltd 1991

Designed and produced by
Aladdin Books Ltd
28 Percy Street
London W1P 0LD

First published in
Great Britain in 1991 by
Watts Books
96 Leonard Street
London EC2A 4RH

Design: David West
        Children's Book
        Design
Designer: Stephen Woosnam-Savage
Editor: Fiona Robertson
Illustrator: Guy Smith
Picture Researcher: Emma Krikler

ISBN 0 7496 0687 8 (Hardback)
      0 7496 2294 6 (Paperback)

Natural Disasters

HURRICANES
AND TYPHOONS

JACQUELINE DINEEN

GLOUCESTER PRESS
London · New York · Toronto · Sydney

CONTENTS

INTRODUCTION

Hurricanes, typhoons and cyclones are the names given to massive tropical storms in different parts of the world. Tropical storms differ from ordinary storms in several important respects. For example, the winds in a tropical storm are always rotational. They whirl round in a circular motion at speeds far greater than those in any ordinary storm. In addition, while the energy unleashed by an ordinary storm is sufficient to provide the whole of the United States with power for 20 minutes, the energy unleashed by a tropical storm is 12,000 times as powerful. Such terrible power has brought death and destruction to many areas of the world, as was shown by the cyclone which battered Bangladesh in April 1991, killing over 250,000 people.

THE WORLD'S WINDS

Winds are caused by movements of warm and cold air. Warm air is lighter than cold air and so rises, creating an area of low pressure at the Earth's surface. In other places cold air sinks down towards the Earth's surface, and spreads out to create an area of high pressure. Winds are therefore movements of air over the Earth's surface from areas of high pressure to areas of low pressure.

At the Equator, where the Sun's rays are strongest, warm air is constantly rising which leads to areas of low pressure. At the poles, the Sun's rays are weaker. Air is cooled over the icy polar caps and sinks to create areas of high pressure. Around the Earth, movements of air between areas of high and low pressure result in the convection cells (right).

The winds are complicated by the spinning of the Earth, which bends the flows of air clockwise in the Northern Hemisphere and anti-clockwise in the Southern Hemisphere. This is known as the Coriolis effect.

▼ **This map shows the prevailing global winds and the breeding grounds in which tropical storms can develop (shaded areas).**

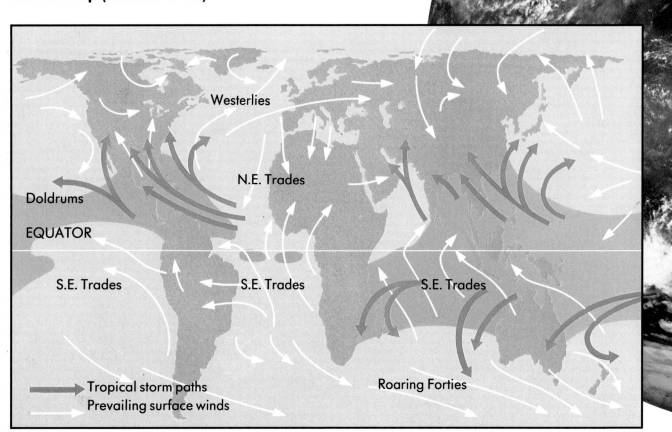

Westerlies

N.E. Trades

Doldrums

EQUATOR

S.E. Trades   S.E. Trades   S.E. Trades

Roaring Forties

→ Tropical storm paths
→ Prevailing surface winds

Wind cells

The heating effect of the Sun on the Earth's surface results in three massive "cells" of rising and falling air. At the Earth's surface, winds blowing from high pressure to low pressure areas are bent by the Coriolis effect.

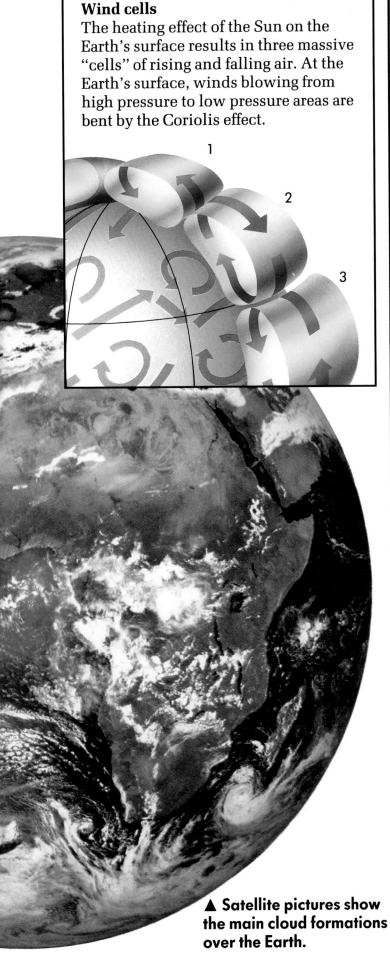

▲ Satellite pictures show the main cloud formations over the Earth.

Clouds

Clouds are formed when air cools to a temperature at which it can no longer hold all its water as vapour. Water droplets are formed, which appear as clouds. The different types of clouds are shown below. Black, heavy cumulonimbus clouds often warn of a storm.

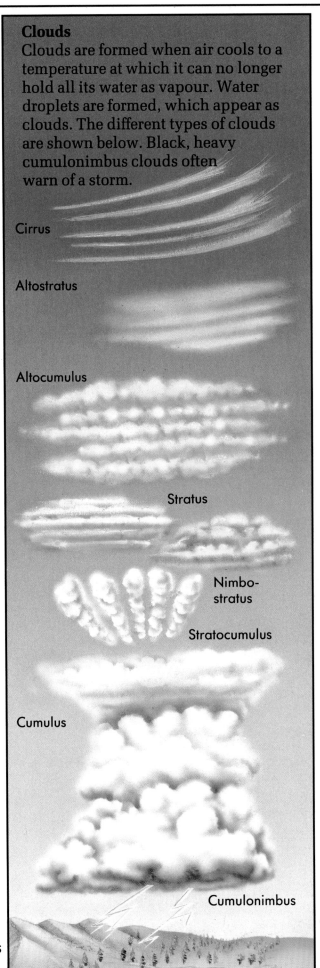

Cirrus

Altostratus

Altocumulus

Stratus

Nimbo-stratus

Stratocumulus

Cumulus

Cumulonimbus

WHAT IS A HURRICANE?

A hurricane is a large spinning wind system which develops over warm seas near the Equator. These areas are known as the tropics. Technically hurricanes are called tropical revolving storms, but they also have local names. They are called hurricanes when they occur over the Atlantic Ocean, typhoons in the Far East and cyclones in the Indian Ocean. By definition, all are characterised by rotating winds which exceed speeds of 120 km/h on the Beaufort Wind Scale.

The tropics are the hottest parts of the world, and experience the most extreme weather conditions. Air heated by the Sun rises very swiftly, which creates areas of very low pressure. As the warm air rises, it becomes loaded with moisture which condenses into massive thunderclouds. Cool air rushes in to fill the void that is left, but because of the constant turning of the Earth on its axis, the air is bent inwards and then spirals upwards with great force. The swirling winds rotate faster and faster, forming a huge circle which can be up to 2,000 km across.

▲ The typhoon which hit Manila in the Philippines in 1988 caused severe flooding. People were forced to cling to items like tyres to survive.

▶ The shattered remains of Darwin in Australia after Cyclone Tracy hit the area on Christmas Day in 1974. Tracy's winds reached 240 km/h and battered the city for over four hours. 48,000 inhabitants were evacuated and 8,000 homes destroyed.

Extreme conditions

A spectacular part of tropical storms are the long, low thunderclouds which can be seen rolling across this landscape. The tinges of grey-black at the edges of the clouds are the result of undercurrents of cold air which force the moisture in the warmer air above to condense very quickly. It is these clouds which bring the torrential downpours of rain that accompany most thunderstorms. Thunder and lightning may also occur.

A HURRICANE BEGINS

Hurricanes usually begin in the steamy late summer in the tropics, when the seas are at their warmest. For a hurricane to develop, the sea surface must have a temperature of at least 26°C. When warm air rises from the seas and condenses into clouds, massive amounts of heat are released. The result of this mixture of heat and moisture is often a collection of thunderstorms, from which a tropical storm can develop.

The trigger for most Atlantic hurricanes is an easterly wave, a band of low pressure moving westwards (see illustration), which may have begun as an African thunderstorm. Vigorous thunderstorms and high winds combine to create a cluster of thunderstorms which can become the seedling for a tropical storm. Typhoons in the Far East and cyclones in the Indian Ocean often develop from a thunderstorm in the equatorial trough (see below). During the hurricane season, the Coriolis effect of the Earth's rotation starts the winds in the thunderstorm spinning in a circular motion.

At the centre of the storm is a calm, cloudless area called the eye, where there is no rain, and the winds are fairly light.

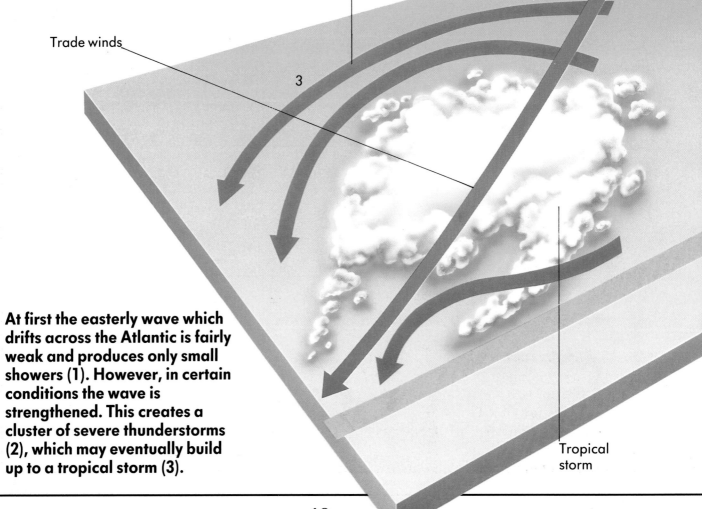

Trade winds

Easterly wave

3

Tropical storm

At first the easterly wave which drifts across the Atlantic is fairly weak and produces only small showers (1). However, in certain conditions the wave is strengthened. This creates a cluster of severe thunderstorms (2), which may eventually build up to a tropical storm (3).

Hurricane detection

The National Hurricane Center (shown right) was formed in 1959 in the United States. One of its aims is to investigate the amount of energy in a hurricane, and to understand the way in which the energy is distributed. Other objectives include studying how hurricanes work, and in what ways their impact could be controlled and reduced. Research is also being carried out concerning the forces that make hurricanes move from the spot where they first begin. Here, hurricane researchers are collecting and analysing data which helps them to identify potential hurricanes.

1

2

Easterly wave

Thunderstorm

Equatorial trough

Seedling storm

► An Atlantic hurricane, photographed from space. The calm, cloudless region of the eye with the fury of the hurricane raging all around it is clearly visible.

THE BUILD UP

As the hurricane builds up it begins to move. It is sustained by a steady flow of warm, moist air. The strongest winds and heaviest rains are found in the towering clouds which merge into a wall about 20-30 km from the storm's centre. Winds around the eye can reach speeds of up to 200 km/h, and a fully developed hurricane pumps out about two million tonnes of air per second. This results in more rain being released in a day than falls in a year on a city like London.

The hurricane travels at speeds of between 15 and 50 km/h. When it hits an area of cold sea or land, it enters a cold, inhospitable climate, where its supply of moist air is cut off. The eye quickly disappears and the storm begins to die down.

Yet it is when it hits the land that a hurricane, typhoon or cyclone causes most damage. Ninety per cent of victims are claimed when the storm first smashes ashore, bringing with it not only powerful winds, but huge waves called storm surges.

Clouds
The clouds are kept swirling round the eye by the strength of the wind. They spin round like a huge catherine wheel.

◄ The air in the eye is calm and smooth at most heights, and is much warmer than that of the surrounding clouds of the hurricane.

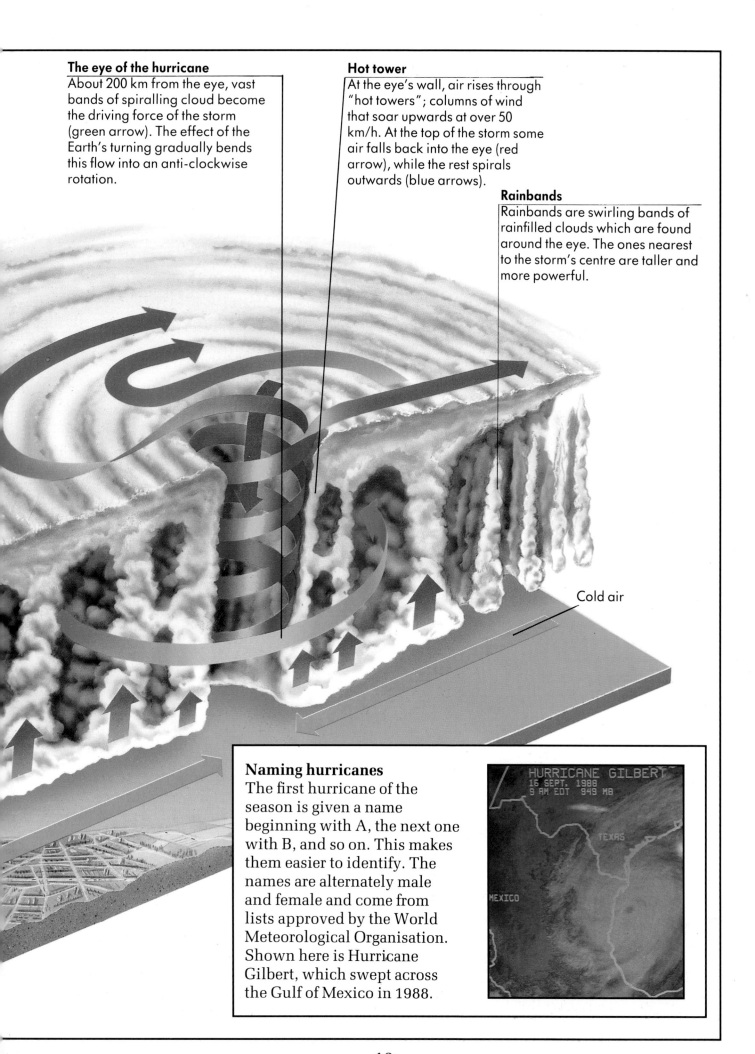

The eye of the hurricane
About 200 km from the eye, vast bands of spiralling cloud become the driving force of the storm (green arrow). The effect of the Earth's turning gradually bends this flow into an anti-clockwise rotation.

Hot tower
At the eye's wall, air rises through "hot towers"; columns of wind that soar upwards at over 50 km/h. At the top of the storm some air falls back into the eye (red arrow), while the rest spirals outwards (blue arrows).

Rainbands
Rainbands are swirling bands of rainfilled clouds which are found around the eye. The ones nearest to the storm's centre are taller and more powerful.

Cold air

Naming hurricanes
The first hurricane of the season is given a name beginning with A, the next one with B, and so on. This makes them easier to identify. The names are alternately male and female and come from lists approved by the World Meteorological Organisation. Shown here is Hurricane Gilbert, which swept across the Gulf of Mexico in 1988.

HURRICANE GILBERT
16 SEPT. 1988
9 AM EDT 949 MB

TEXAS

MEXICO

THE STORM SURGE

The deadly companion of every tropical storm is the storm surge; the huge mounds of sea water that are whipped up by the powerful winds.

The first sign of a storm surge can occur nearly a week before the actual hurricane, typhoon or cyclone. Winds move outwards much faster than the storm itself and whip up the sea into waves up to 1.5 m high along the coastline. When the storm is about 180 km from land, huge waves driven by its winds begin to crash ashore. The deafening roar of the waves' surf can be heard miles inland. This is followed by the most deadly and destructive element of the surge as the bulge of water which forms beneath the storm's eye smashes ashore.

The effects of such storm surges are far-reaching. Low-lying coastal areas can be devastated by the severe floods that result, and many lives and homes may be lost. In the Far East, typhoons build up in the western Pacific Ocean and batter Japan and the Asian mainland. Cyclones that begin in the Indian Ocean can veer south towards East Africa.

Storm surges

A storm surge builds up out at sea as a tropical storm races in towards the shore. The sea level rises above the height of protective sand dunes on the shore. As the sea rushes in, it flattens the dunes and swamps the land behind them. This town will be flooded by the storm surge.

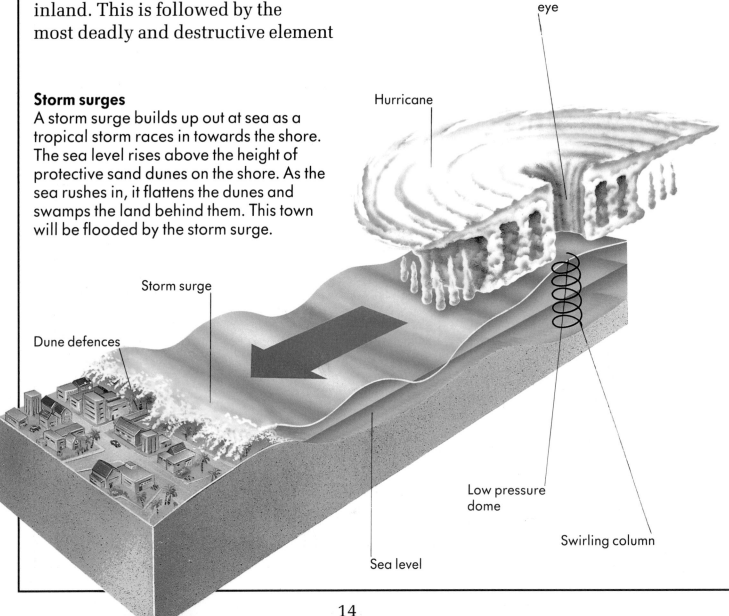

Hurricane's eye

Hurricane

Storm surge

Dune defences

Low pressure dome

Swirling column

Sea level

Into the storm
The unpredictability of tropical storms and the speed with which they can suddenly change course have caught the crews of many ships at sea unawares.
Equipped to deal with such emergencies are tug boats like the "Abeille-Languedoc" (shown right), which often have to undertake rescue missions arising from storms at sea.

Sea storms in history

For ships at sea, no storm poses a greater threat than a fully-developed hurricane or winds of hurricane force. Although sailing ships were built to withstand gales and storms, the winds and mountainous seas created by such extreme weather phenomena often caused great damage. In this illustration, desperate sailors are seen trying to stay afloat as their ships sink in the maelstrom of the English Channel. This storm was one of the worst in England's history. It struck in November 1703 and its hurricane-force winds claimed about 8,000 lives and destroyed more than 14,000 homes.

▲ A US destroyer caught in the enormous waves formed by a typhoon in December, 1944. The storm was so severe that the waves were described by the captain of the ship as being "like vertical mountains".

A FREAK ON LAND

In many ways, a tornado resembles a miniature hurricane. However, tornadoes are far more powerful than hurricanes. This is because their fearsome energy is concentrated into a violently spinning column of air less than a kilometre across.

Unlike hurricanes, tornadoes tend to form over the land. Central North America experiences more tornadoes than anywhere else in the world. They usually occur during cloudy, stormy weather and descend from a severe thunderstorm as a rapidly-spinning white funnel of cloud. Dust and soil are drawn up into the funnel in a spiral which can be seen hurtling across the landscape. A screaming roar pierces the ears and scythe-like winds cut through even the strongest of buildings. Cars, caravans and even aeroplanes have been picked up, carried away and then dropped and smashed like toys.

When it touches the ground the tornado quickly turns grey with dust and develops ragged edges. It becomes weaker, can no longer suck up the air in its path, and gradually dies out.

The ultimate storm

Tornadoes are the strongest winds in the world and can often cause total destruction of the area they hit. As the tornado's funnel tightens, the winds begin to spin faster and faster. The rotating winds pick up dust and debris, and the tornado is surrounded by an envelope of dust. Inside the dust envelope, the strongest winds can be found rotating at speeds of up to 300 km/h around a calm, central eye of low pressure. This is known as the funnel cloud. Because the tornado's lowest pressure is near the ground, air that is sucked up into the funnel at first gains speed as it spirals around the eye. The air gradually slows down and spreads out as it reaches the heavy cumulonimbus clouds which are found at the top of the tornado.

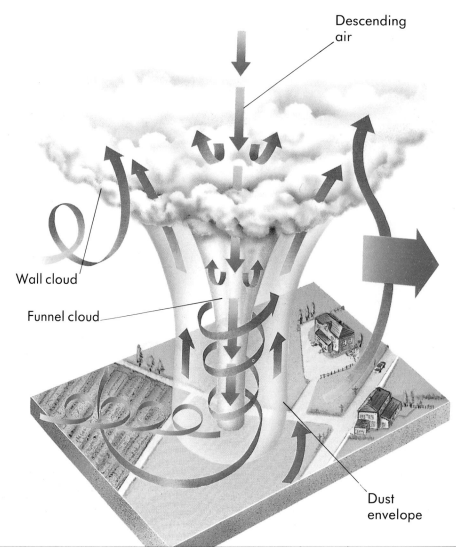

Descending air

Wall cloud

Funnel cloud

Dust envelope

A waterspout is a funnel of air which extends down from a cloud over the sea. In the same way as a tornado sucks up soil and debris, the waterspout sucks up great quantities of water. This gives the funnel its dark colour (right). Waterspouts are much weaker than tornadoes and their winds rarely exceed speeds of 80 km/h. They only last for about 15 minutes and occur mainly in shallow coastal waters.

THE DAMAGE

For anyone caught in a hurricane, the experience is a terrifying one. Fierce, whirling winds rip across the countryside, overturning cars and heavy lorries. Trees are ripped from the ground by their roots, and whole buildings can be lifted from their foundations.

Some of the worst disasters occur near coastal areas, where stormy seas contribute to the havoc that is wreaked. In 1938, one of the most powerful hurricanes in history swept through Long Island, New York. In just seven hours, the storm killed at least 600 people and destroyed the homes of over 60,000. The total damage was estimated at the enormous sum of one third of a billion dollars. The storm destroyed 26,000 cars and 47,000 km of electric, telegraph and telephone wires and flooded thousands of hectares of land.

One coastal area on the island was so badly hit by the hurricane that 200 homes there were completely swept away. Rescue workers searching for missing people had to use maps from telephone companies to identify the sites on which the houses once stood.

▲ The storm surge that hit Bangladesh's low lying deltas in 1991 claimed hundreds of thousands of lives.

◄▼ When Hurricane Hugo hit Puerto Rico in 1989, 15 were killed and over 50,000 left homeless. Roofs were blown off, buildings demolished, and low-lying areas flooded by the torrential rains and high waves.

PLOTTING THE PATH

No one can do anything to prevent a hurricane. The only thing weather forecasters can do is to try and plot the hurricane's path. People living in the area can then be warned and evacuated if necessary.

Weather stations all over the world exchange information about winds, rainfall, cloud, temperature and air pressure. Satellites in space circle the Earth and take photographs of the atmosphere from above, which can be used to show how clouds are forming.

At the first signs that a tropical storm is building up, information can be fed into computers to try to predict its course. First a band of low-pressure may develop over tropical seas, in an area which has spawned tropical storms in the past. For example, storms near the west coast of Africa have led to violent hurricanes and storm surges which later hit the islands of the Caribbean. In 1985, hurricane experts in the United States spotted a storm of this type and plotted its course as it developed into Hurricane Gloria. One million people had to be evacuated from their homes on the east coast of the United States.

▼ **The colours on infra-red pictures of tropical storms help meteorologists to measure temperature and rainfall in different parts of the hurricane, and to estimate the storm's strength and course.**

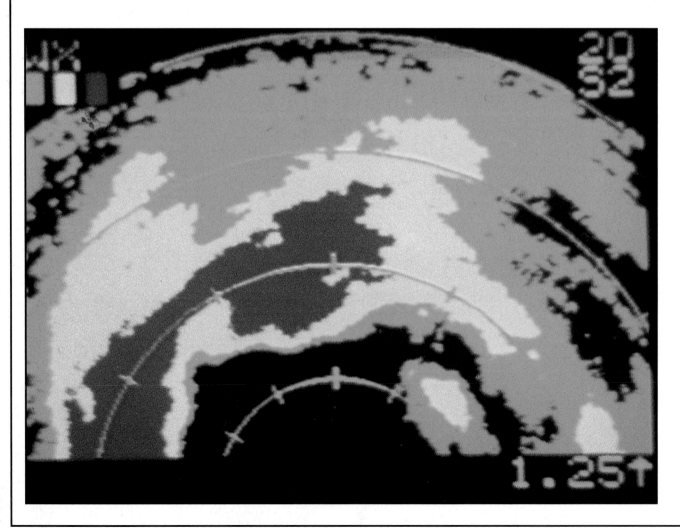

► Scientists at Colorado's Environmental Research Laboratories are combining sophisticated new instruments with computer technology to create a new "minute by minute" weather warning system. The system uses special radar devices, called profilers, which are directed towards the sky. Sophisticated computer equipment and other monitoring systems are also used. In this way, changes in the atmosphere can be quickly detected, and storms can be recognised even as they are forming. The storm's movement is then charted on screens (shown right).

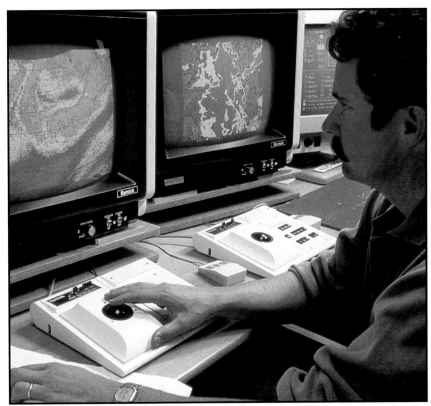

▼ Satellites in space play a major role in helping scientists to investigate and understand the changes in climate which lead to extreme weather conditions like tropical storms. The satellites map ocean waves, currents and tides, as well as sea-surface temperatures and winds around the world.

GETTING IT WRONG

The United States is often battered by hurricanes, but the countries of Europe rarely find themselves in the path of such violent storms.

In the autumn of 1987, however, a freak storm with hurricane-force winds swept across the Atlantic from the United States. Although the storm was not a fully-developed hurricane with swirling, rotating winds, it nevertheless wreaked havoc in the countries it hit. The winds strengthened as they approached Europe. First Spain and Portugal were battered by strong gales. Forecasters expected the winds to die down before they reached Britain, but their predictions were wrong. The winds became stronger still as they blew on towards northern France and southern England.

The full force of the storm struck in the middle of the night, as everyone slept. Had the storm arrived during the day, many more people would probably have been killed. As it was, the main damage was to buildings and trees. Thousands of trees were uprooted like matchsticks and thrown across roads and over cars and buildings. Many roads were blocked by the fallen debris. Roofs and chimneys were blown off and flying roof slates and tiles hurtled through the air. Some buildings collapsed, and millions of people were without power for several days because of damage to power lines.

▲ Huge waves battered the coast of Normandy as the storm crossed northern France. For four days, rising tides spilled sea-water over nearby farmland, destroying crops and livestock and rendering the land useless for at least the next five years.

The hurricanes that move inland

In 1954, Hurricane Hazel swept across the Caribbean Sea and intensified as it hit the east coast of the United States. The hurricane brought torrential rains and record winds to many areas, including Maryland, Virginia and New York City. In Washington, government workers were allowed to go home early. Many had to cling to lamp posts for support against the high winds as they tried to cross the road (shown below).

▼ The storm that battered Europe in 1987 caused millions of pounds worth of damage to property. In England, the south coast suffered most storm damage.

LIVING WITH THE THREAT

The threat of hurricanes is an ever-present one. Even if precautions are taken, they can still cause misery and devastation.

However, some countries are too poor to take precautions, and unfortunately, it is often these areas which are hit most severely by tropical storms. Bangladesh is in southern Asia. It is one of the world's poorest countries, and about 100 million people eke out a living by farming the fertile mudflats at the mouth of the Ganges River. This area is often hit by violent cyclones, such as the one which swept through the area in April 1991. Thousands of people have been killed as massive storm surges swept over them and their flimsy homes. Those who do survive have no homes and no food or clean water. In such conditions diseases such as cholera quickly spread, making the death toll higher.

Building defences

Sea walls are the best protection for towns near the sea. Some walls have tops that curve outwards so that the waves are turned back on themselves as they break against them. Others have teeth or ridges which are designed to break up the wave and reduce its impact. When floods do occur, efficient pumping stations are needed to get rid of the water quickly. Shutters can be used to protect windows from smashing. The window in the picture below has been covered with strips of tape to stop it from shattering.

Clearing up the mess

The damage caused by a hurricane can take months or even years to repair. People are often forced to salvage what little they have left from their flooded or wrecked homes (below right). Roads have to be cleared and fallen debris removed (below). Electricity and phone lines have to be repaired. Emergency food and water supplies may have to be brought in to the affected area. After Hurricane Hugo struck Puerto Rico, power stations there were so badly damaged that three-quarters of homes in the area were without power. Oil storage tanks were also badly damaged (photo bottom).

ARE WE CAUSING MORE?

Hurricanes are sustained by warm, moist air. The countries of northern Europe have a fairly cool climate. So why have they been hit by hurricanes in recent years?

One theory is that global warming is having some effect. As the planet heats up, more parts of the world are developing the kind of climate which is ideal for tropical storms.

The gases in the Earth's atmosphere act like the glass of a greenhouse, trapping enough heat from the Sun to keep the planet warm enough for life. This is known as the "Greenhouse Effect". One of the main greenhouse gases is carbon dioxide. Other greenhouse gases are methane, water vapour and chlorofluorocarbons (CFCs). The only way we can prevent global warming is by controlling the amounts of these gases that are released into the atmosphere.

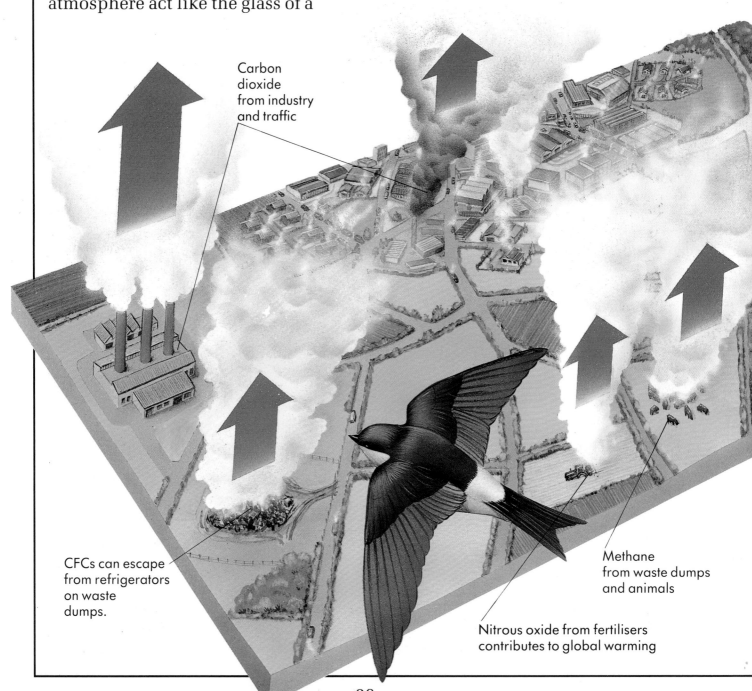

Carbon dioxide from industry and traffic

CFCs can escape from refrigerators on waste dumps.

Methane from waste dumps and animals

Nitrous oxide from fertilisers contributes to global warming

The Greenhouse Effect

The atmosphere allows sunlight through to heat the Earth, but traps some of the heat that radiates back towards space. This is rather like the way the glass in a greenhouse works, and so is called the Greenhouse Effect. The gases which prevent some of the heat from escaping into space are known as greenhouse gases. They help to maintain the right temperatures on Earth for life. If too many greenhouse gases are present however, too much warmth is trapped, which could make global temperatures rise.

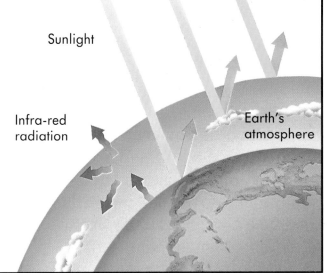

Sunlight

Infra-red radiation

Earth's atmosphere

Water vapour

▶ Carbon dioxide occurs naturally in the atmosphere, but is also produced by burning fuels in factories and power stations, and is emitted in traffic exhaust fumes. Plants absorb carbon dioxide, but clearing large areas of rainforests means there are fewer plants to do this. Levels of carbon dioxide in the atmosphere therefore increase.

WHAT CAN WE DO?

In the rich, industrialised countries, meteorologists are working on ways of improving information and warning systems, and of pinpointing danger zones. However, even when sophisticated equipment is used, and information is processed by computer, hurricanes can still take people by surprise. If the storm suddenly changes course, the evacuation of an area may not be possible. Precautions should therefore be taken to reduce the impact of the hurricane, typhoon or cyclone and to offer protection for people in its path.

In low-lying areas, special shelters can be built for this purpose. Bangladesh has 63 cyclone shelters. They are raised four metres from the ground and built to withstand even greater forces than those experienced during the latest cyclone. Each shelter can hold up to 1,500 people, but about 350,000 people made use of them during the latest disaster.

Preventing global warming

There are several ways to reduce the amount of harmful greenhouse gases currently being pumped into the atmosphere. For example, to reduce carbon dioxide levels, we must start by burning less fossil fuels, both in industry (below) and at home.

This can be done by using alternative sources of energy, like wind, water and solar power, which do not release carbon dioxide into the atmosphere. Homes and factories can be made more efficient so they use less energy. And forests can be replanted to stop carbon dioxide building up in the atmosphere.

► Teams of hurricane experts around the world gather information about changes in the weather. Warnings and progress reports can be issued every few hours via radio and television once a possible storm has been identified.

▼ Scientists use planes like the one shown below to journey into the eye of the hurricane. The plane's probe, which is located in front of the nose, gives instant information on the pressure and humidity inside the hurricane, thereby enabling scientists to calculate its strength.

FACT FILE

The cyclones that hit Bangladesh

Bangladesh has been the victim of many cyclones which cause flooding of the Ganges delta. In 1970, a tropical cyclone claimed 500,000 lives there. Thousands died in 1985 when a massive wall of water swept over the mudflats where people lived and farmed the land.

In April 1991, a devastating cyclone raced into the Bay of Bengal at 230 km/h, and waves nearly seven metres high flooded many communities on the coast. It is thought that 250,000 people may have been killed, some of them on fishing boats and others in flimsy houses made of mud and straw. This is the worst cyclone to hit Bangladesh this century, with stronger winds than the 1970 storm. Warnings were given, but many people did not have radios or television so they did not hear them. Others did not believe the cyclone would hit them because there had been several false alarms. About 10 million people were left homeless. They had no food and only muddy, salty water to drink. Millions more people may die from starvation and diseases such as cholera.

Tropical storms in history

1737 Cyclone storm surge killed 300,000 people in the Calcutta area of India.
1899 300 people killed in Bathurst, Queensland by a 15 m storm surge, formed as a result of cyclone winds.
1900 A hurricane and storm surge hit Galveston, Texas, in the United States, causing about 6,000 deaths.
1945 2,000 people killed by a typhoon in Japan – just 42 days after the devastation of Hiroshima by a nuclear bomb.
1953 307 people killed by hurricane force winds. A storm surge was created which washed over the east coast of England. The same surge claimed over 1,800 lives in Holland.
1963 Hurricane Flora killed 5,000 people on the island of Haiti in the Caribbean.
1969 Hurricane Camille caused destruction from Louisiana to Virginia, in the United States, killing 250 people.
1970 Hurricane Celia killed 11 people on the Texas coast in America.
500,000 were killed by a cyclone in Bangladesh.
1972 122 people from Florida to New York were killed by floods during Hurricane Agnes.
1974 About 8,000 people were killed by Hurricane Fifi in Honduras, Central America.
1974 Cyclone Tracy flattened the city of Darwin in Australia.
1976 Hurricane Liza killed 400 people in Mexico.
1979 Hurricane David hit Puerto Rico and the south-east coast of America, causing 4,000 deaths.
1980 Hurricane Allen hit the Caribbean Islands, killing 272 people.
1983 Hurricane Alicia killed 21 people in Galveston, Texas.

Tornado terrors

The United States has more than 850 tornadoes a year. Most tornadoes happen between April and October. The most disastrous in terms of lives lost was in the mid-western states in 1925, when 689 people were killed. But others have had devastating consequences too. In April 1979, a tornado struck the city of Wichita Falls in Texas. By the time it had passed, the city looked as though it had been bombed: 20,000 people were left homeless and 46 were killed. Sometimes several tornadoes start at once. In 1974, 148 tornadoes killed 315 people in 13 states over a period of two days. In April 1991, a series of tornadoes ripped through the states of Kansas and Oklahoma, flattening hundreds of homes and destroying a caravan park containing 400 mobile homes. Hundreds of people were injured and more than 30 people were killed.

The highest storm surge

The highest storm surge was in 1969 during Hurricane Camille, when a wave 7.6 metres high flooded the coast at Pass Christian, Mississippi.

GLOSSARY

air pressure – the weight of the air in the lower layers of the atmosphere pressing down on the Earth. This is always changing as air moves around. Warm air rises and expands. It becomes thinner and lighter, so it does not press down on the Earth so hard, creating an area of low pressure. Low pressure areas, or "lows", bring cloudy, rainy weather because the air high up cools and moisture condenses into clouds. As the cool air descends again, it becomes heavier, so it is at high pressure. The air warms up as it sinks, and clouds disappear. So a "high" often brings dry, clear weather.

atmosphere – the envelope of gases that surround the Earth. The atmosphere protects us from the Sun and also provides us with the oxygen we need to breathe.

Beaufort Scale – a scale of wind speeds which is based on things which can be easily seen, such as smoke, trees and damage caused. The Beaufort numbers range between 0 and 12, grading winds from calm to hurricane force. The scale was devised by Admiral Sir Francis Beaufort and is the official method of describing wind speeds.

condense – to turn from water vapour into tiny drops of water. You can see this happening to steam from a kettle when it hits a cold surface such as a wall or window.

cyclone – the name for tropical storms when they occur in the Indian Ocean.

delta – a fan-shaped area of land which is formed when a river deposits large amounts of silt at its mouth. The river divides into separate channels as it flows through the delta to the sea.

evacuate – to remove people from a place which is considered to be dangerous.

eye – the calm, cloudless centre of a hurricane, cyclone, or typhoon.

front – the boundary between a mass of warm, moist air and a mass of cold, dry air.

global warming – the heating up of the Earth by a build-up of carbon dioxide and other "greenhouse" gases in the atmosphere. Heat cannot escape back into space and so the Greenhouse Effect is increased. This may cause the planet to warm up, possibly to a dangerous degree.

hemisphere – half a sphere. The Equator divides the Earth into the Northern Hemisphere and the Southern Hemisphere.

meteorologist – someone who studies information about weather conditions and prepares a weather forecast.

monsoon – the rainy season in India and south-east Asia. In the summer, moist winds blow in from the Indian Ocean, bringing heavy rain. In the autumn, cool, dry winds blow out from the land, bringing dry weather.

satellite – a small object moving around a larger one, such as the Moon moving around the Earth. Weather satellites are man-made devices which orbit the Earth and send back weather information.

storm surge – massive waves which build up out at sea as a tropical storm blows in.

temperate – describes a climate which has four seasons, spring, summer, autumn and winter.

thermal current – a current of air which is rising because it has been heated.

tropics – the part of the Earth between the Tropic of Cancer and the Tropic of Capricorn. The weather is hottest at the Equator.

typhoon – the name for tropical storms when they occur in the Far East.

INDEX

Photographic credits:
Cover, title page and pages 4-5, 8, 11 top and bottom, 12, 13, 15 top, 18-19 all, 20, 21 top and bottom right, 22, 24 left and right, 25 all and 29 top and bottom: Frank Spooner Pictures; pages 6-7 and 21 bottom left: Science Photo Library; pages 8-9 and 27: Frank Lane Picture Agency; page 9: Hutchison Library; page 15 bottom left: Mary Evans Picture Library; page 15 bottom right: Popperfoto; pages 17 top, 22-23 bottom and 28: Spectrum Colour Library; page 17 bottom: Robert Harding Picture Library; page 23 top: Topham Picture Source.